Flute

CONTENTS

Two Worlds 4

You'll Be in My Heart..............................6

Son of Man 8

Trashin' the Camp 12

Strangers Like Me 14

ISBN 0-634-01059-X

Walt Disney Music Company

DISTRIBUTED BY

7777 W. BLUEMOUND RD. P.O. BOX 13819 MILWAUKEE, WI 53213

Two Worlds

4

FLUTE

Words and Music by
PHIL COLLINS

You'll Be in My Heart

(Pop Version)

Words and Music by
PHIL COLLINS

FLUTE

Son of Man

FLUTE

Words and Music by
PHIL COLLINS

Trashin' the Camp

FLUTE

Words and Music by
PHIL COLLINS

Moderate Swing (quarter note = 104) (two eighths = triplet quarter–eighth)

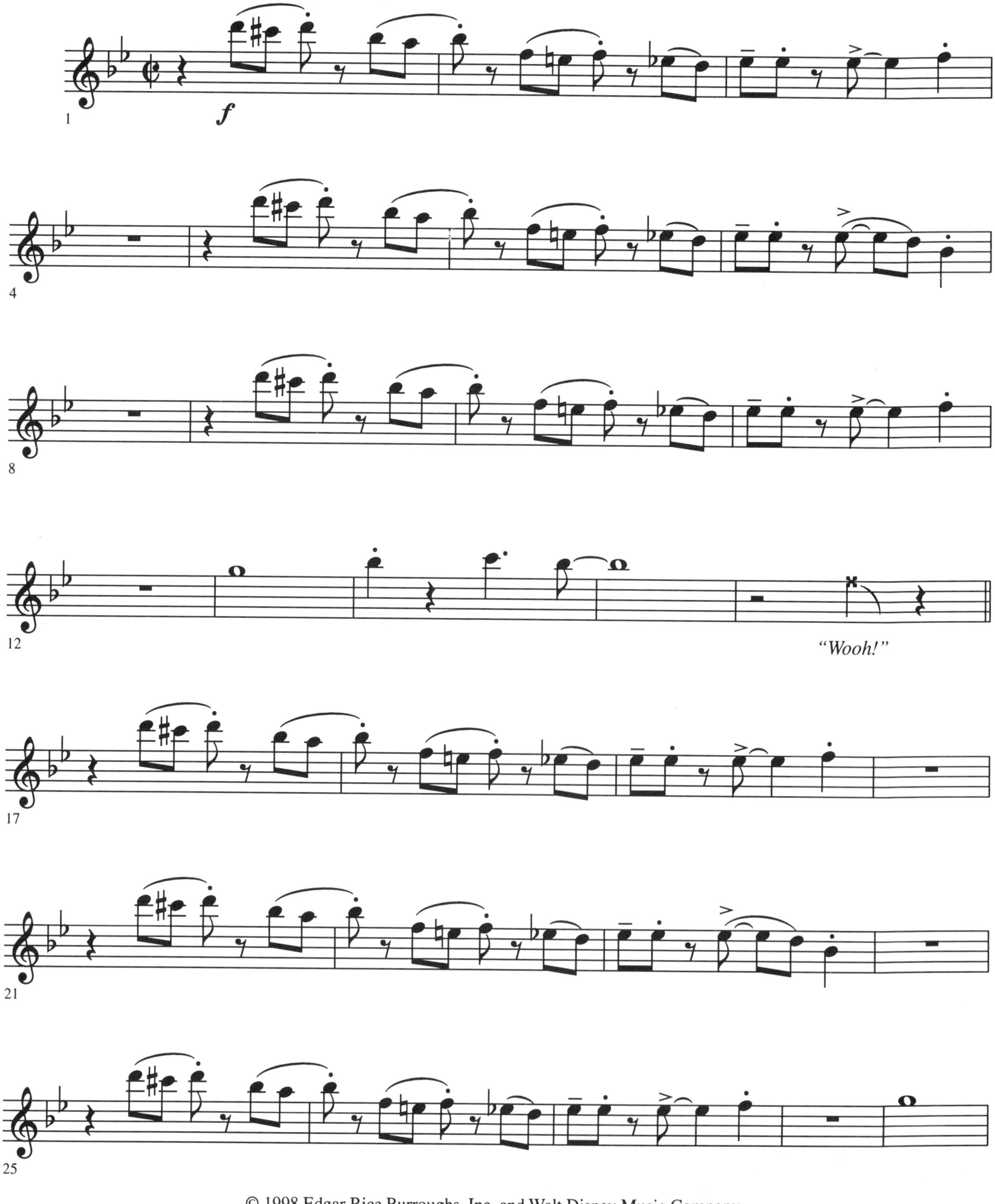

30

"Wooh!"

35

40

43

47

51

Gradually faster

56 "Wooh!"

60 "Wooh!"   "Wooh!"

64 "Wooh!"   "Wooh!"   "Wooh!"

Strangers Like Me

FLUTE

Words and Music by
PHIL COLLINS